Positively beYOUtiful Vibes!

Char Green

4Him

ISBN: 9781072087595

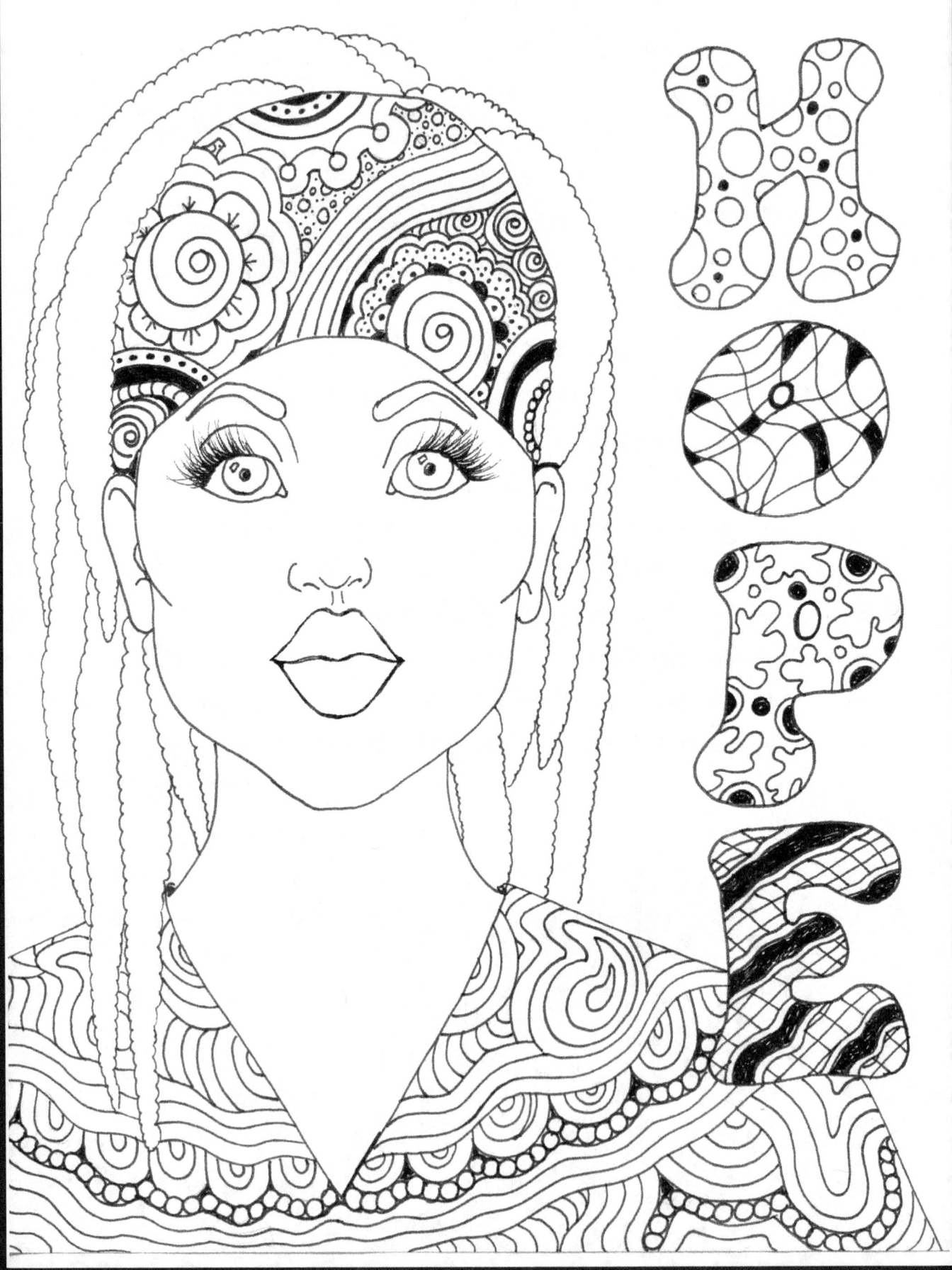

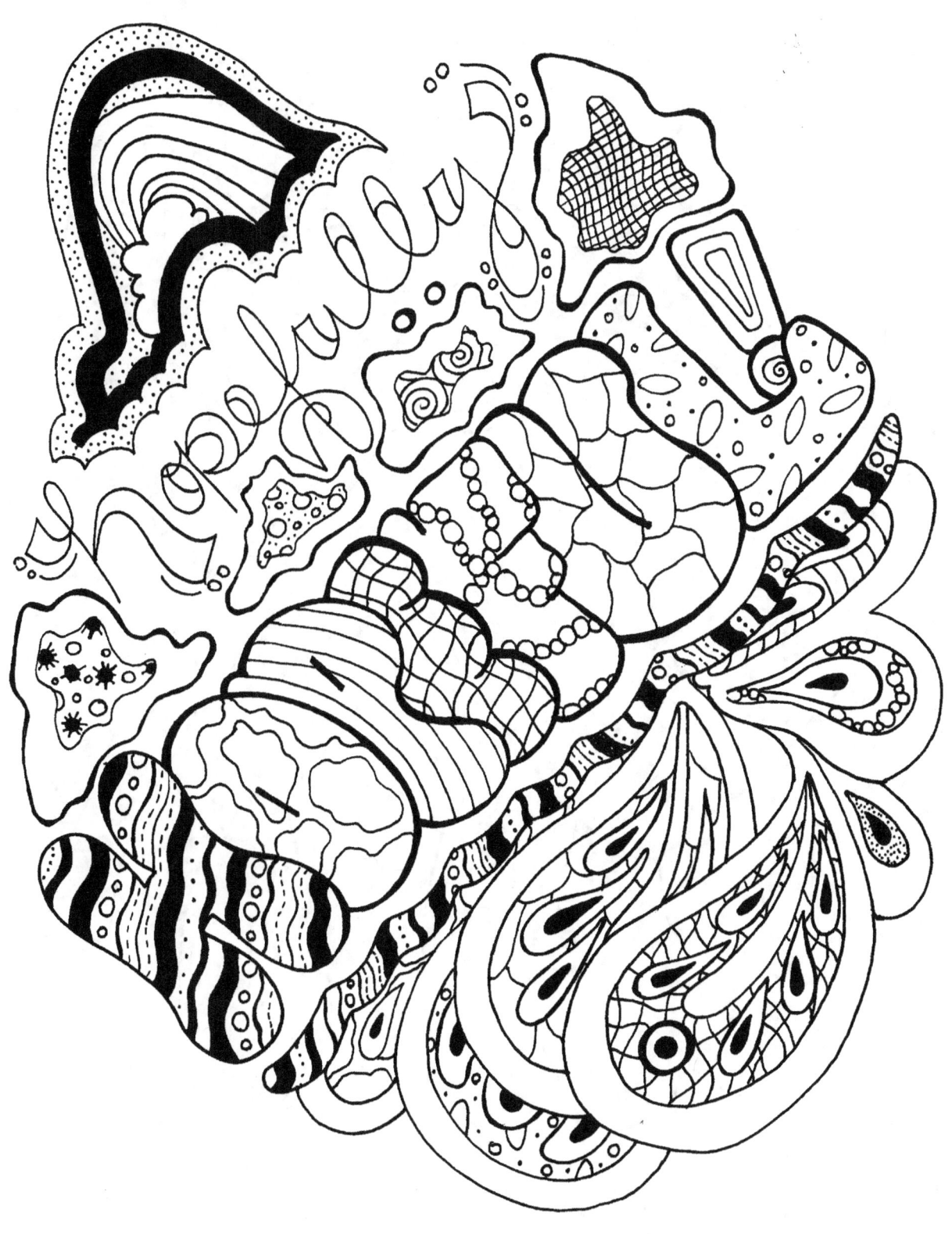

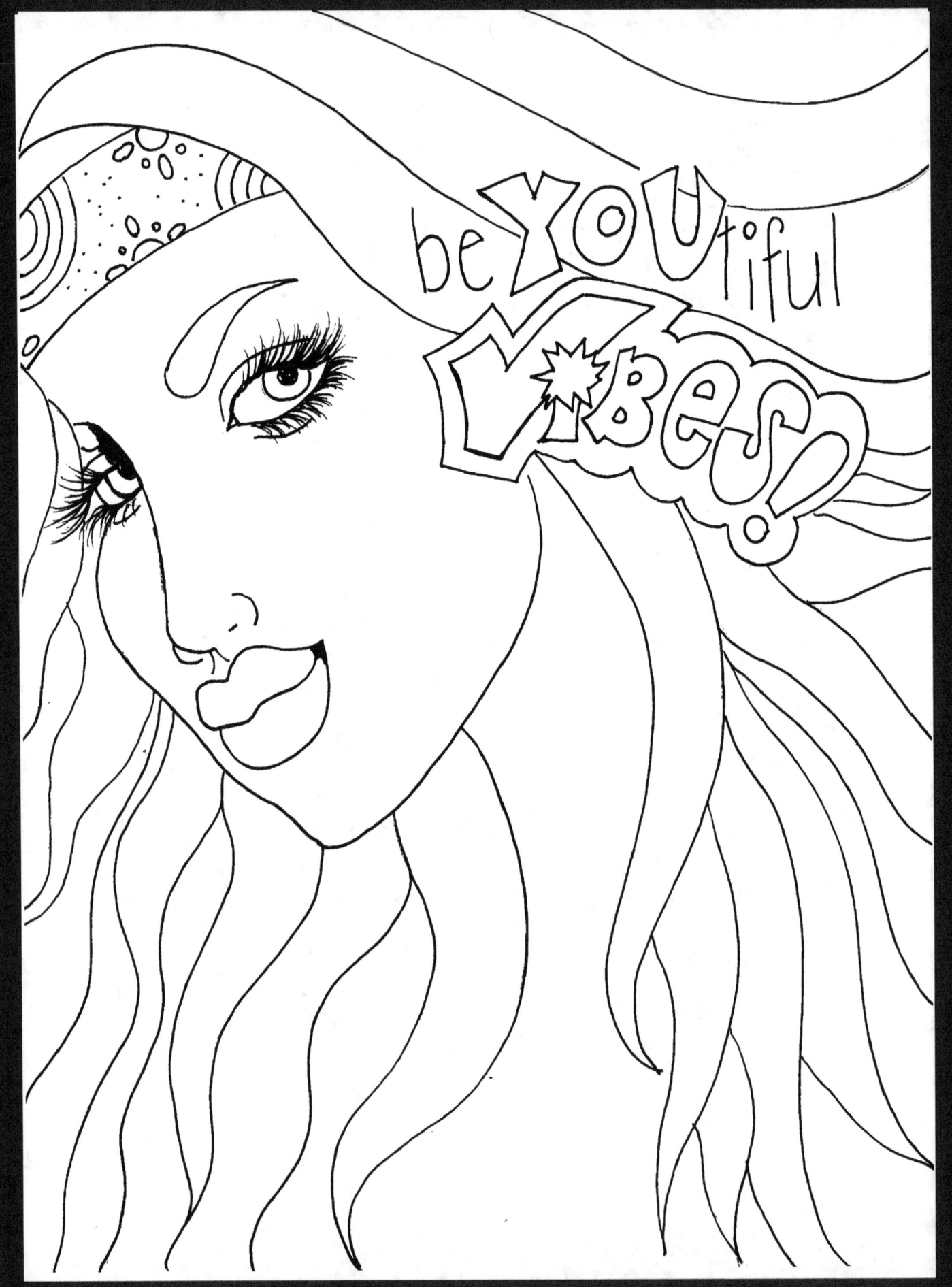

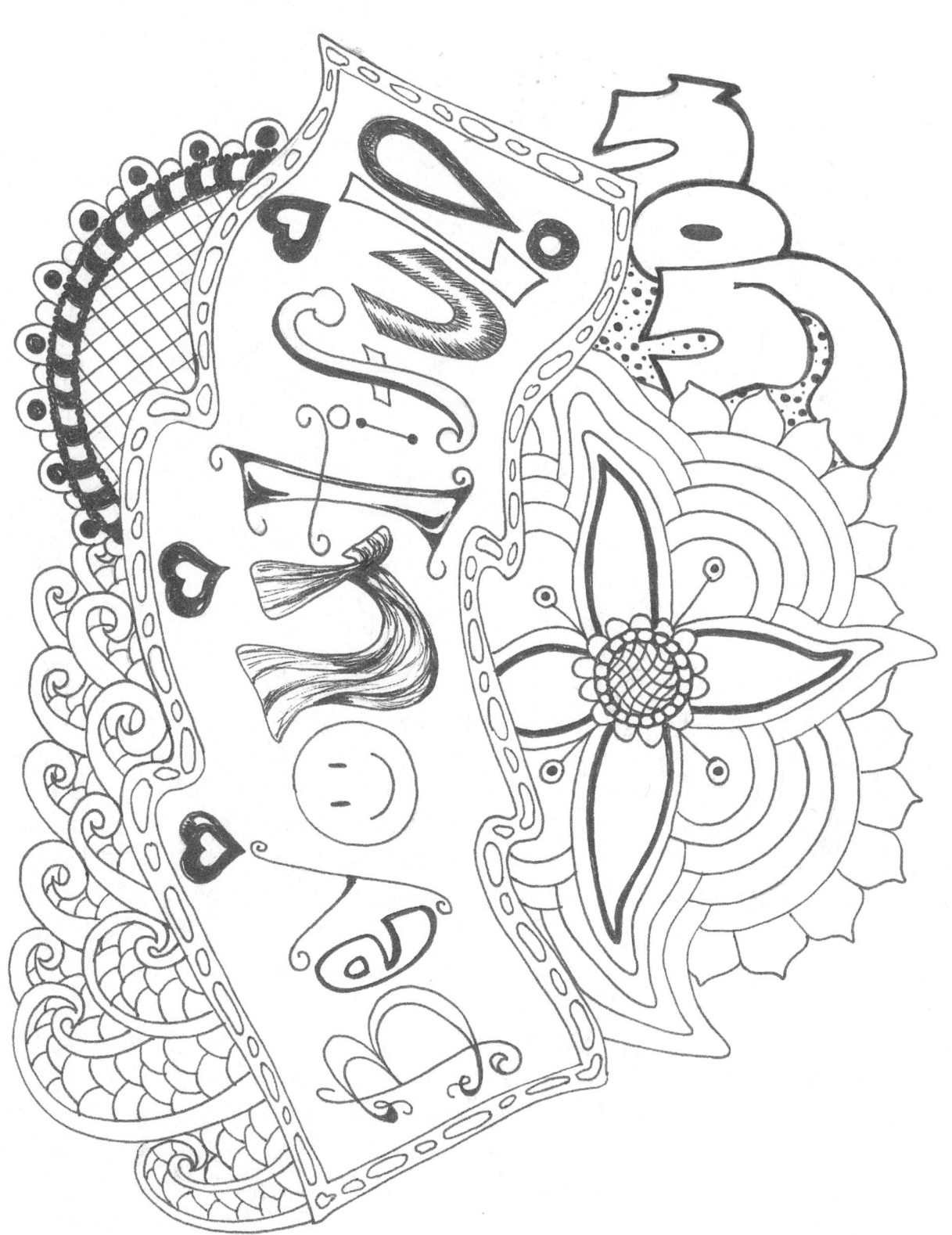

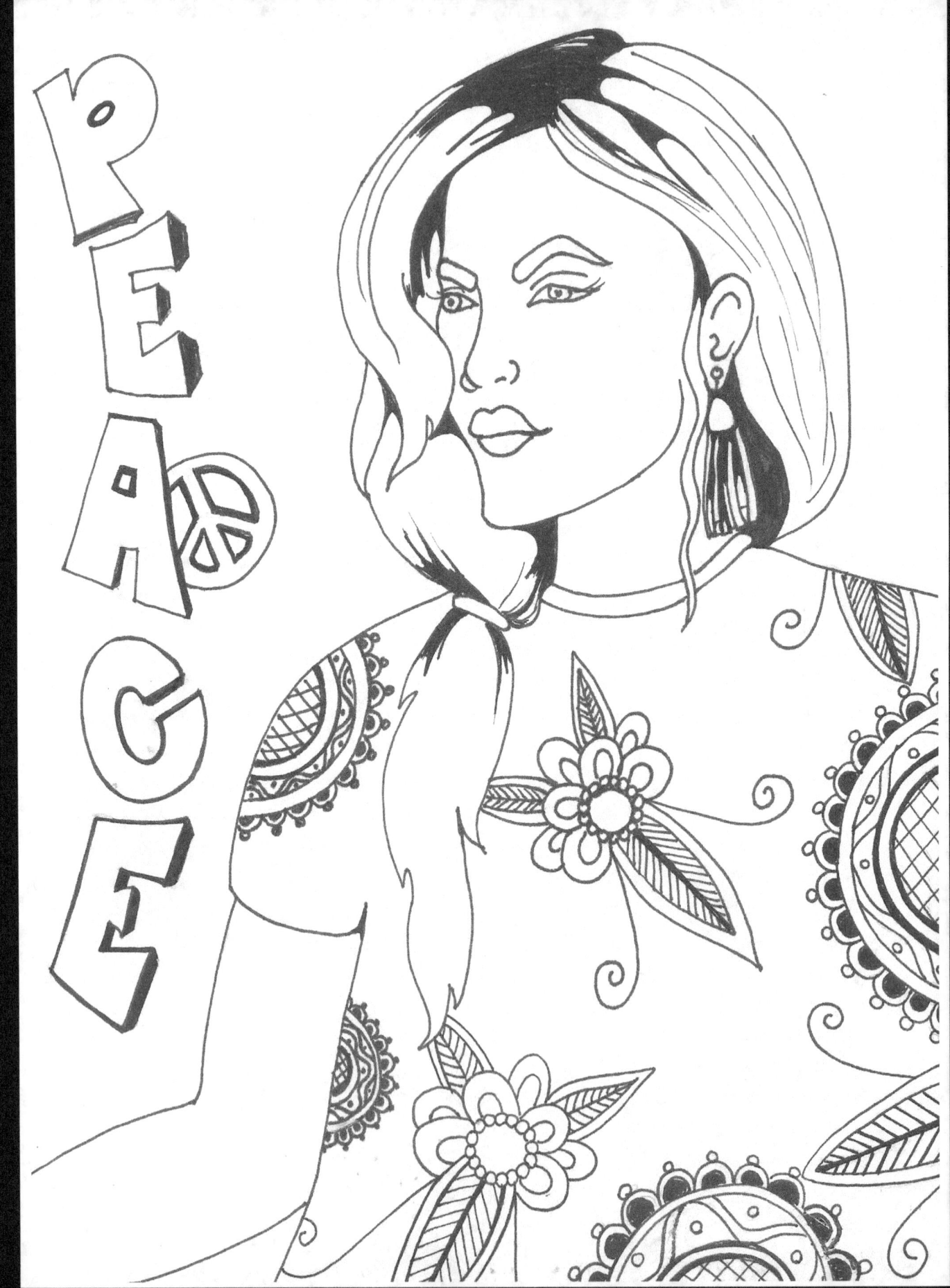

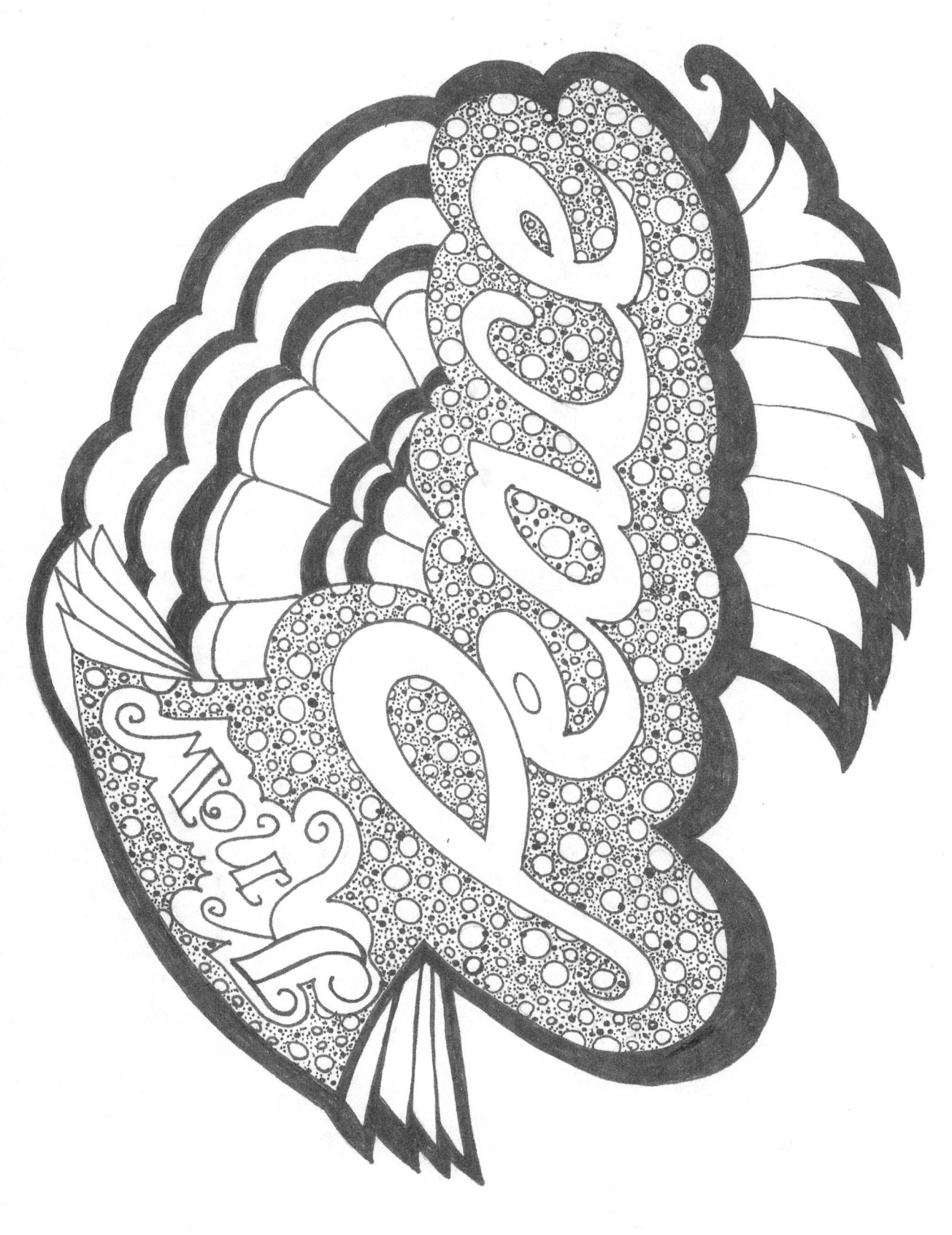

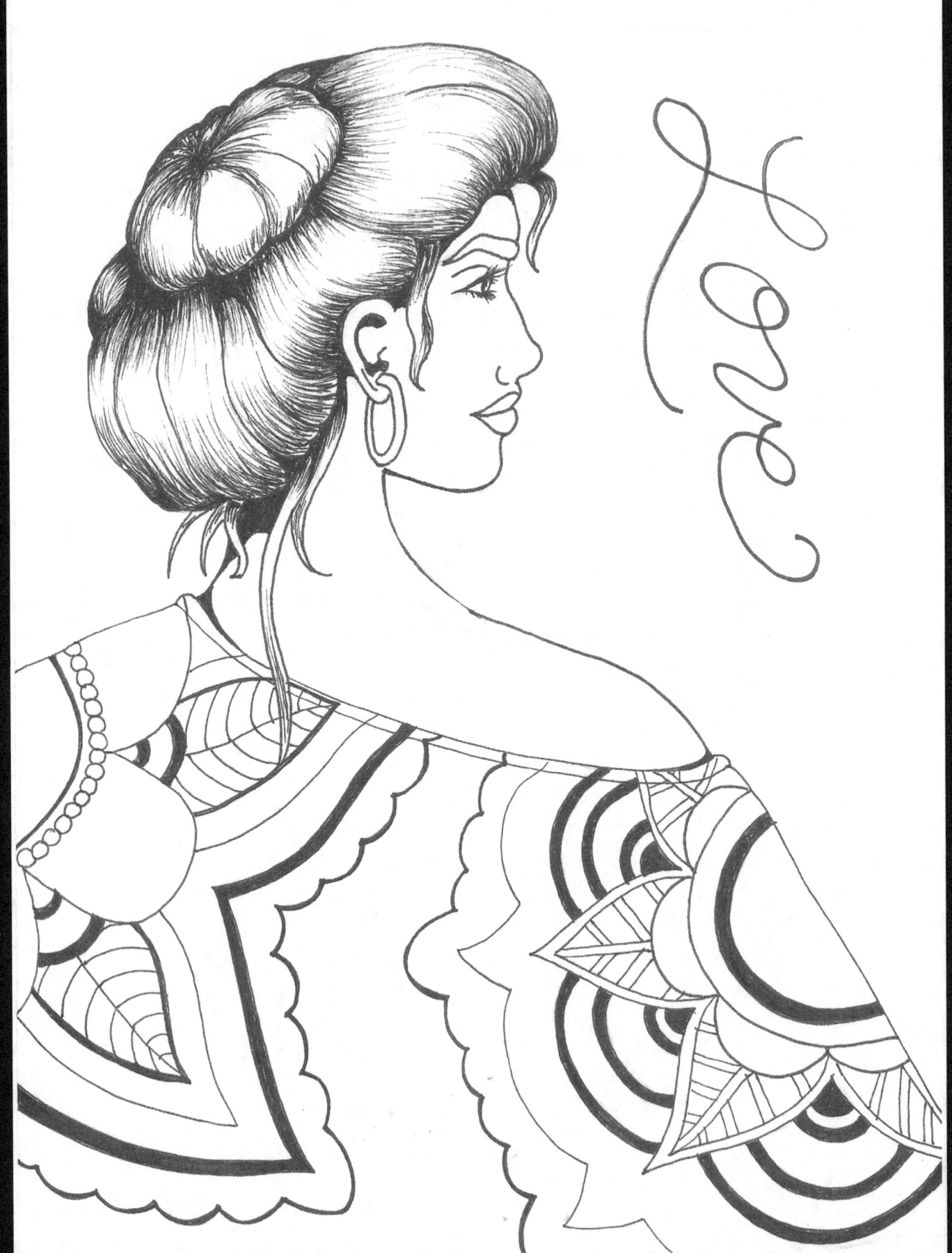

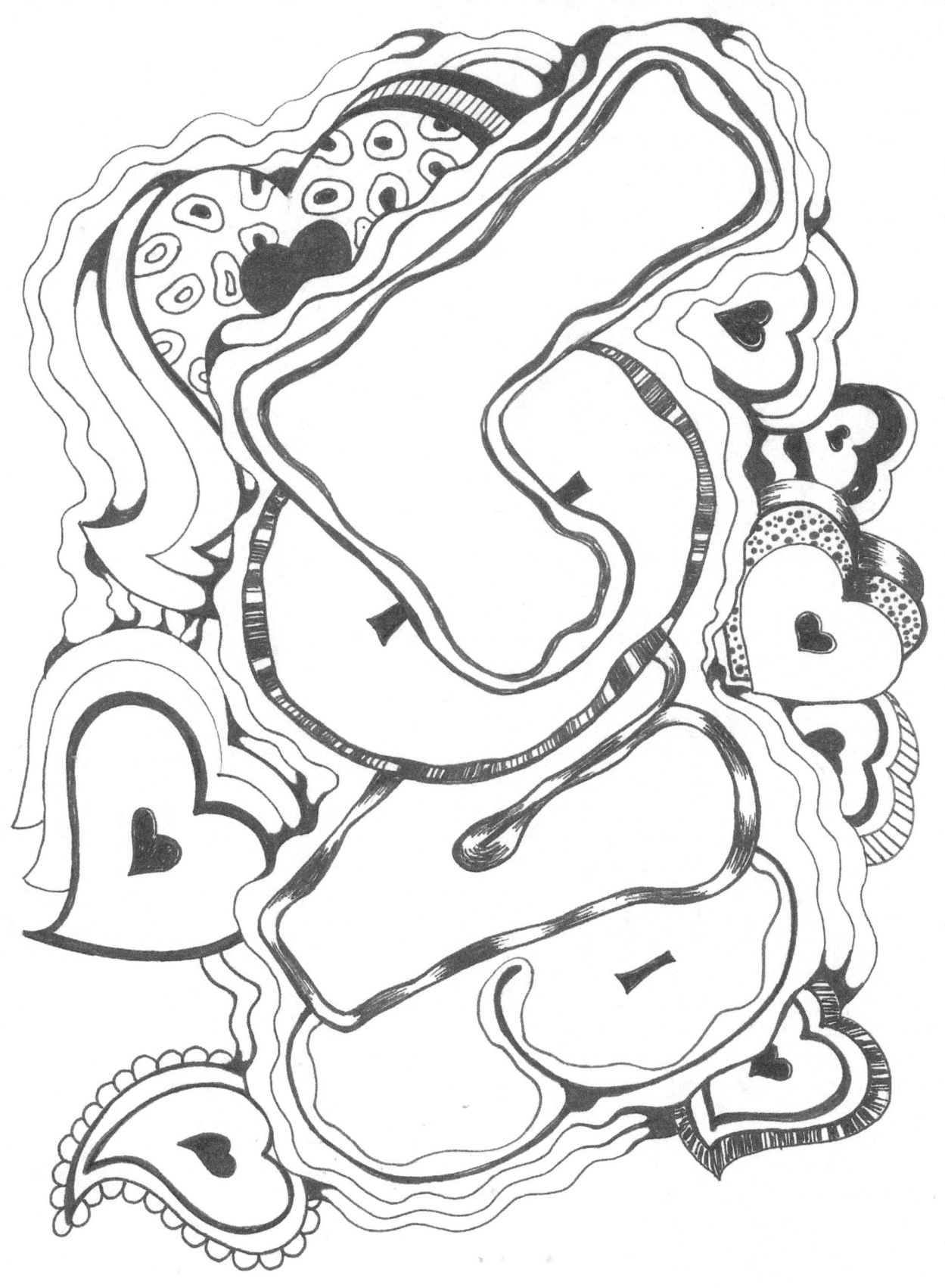

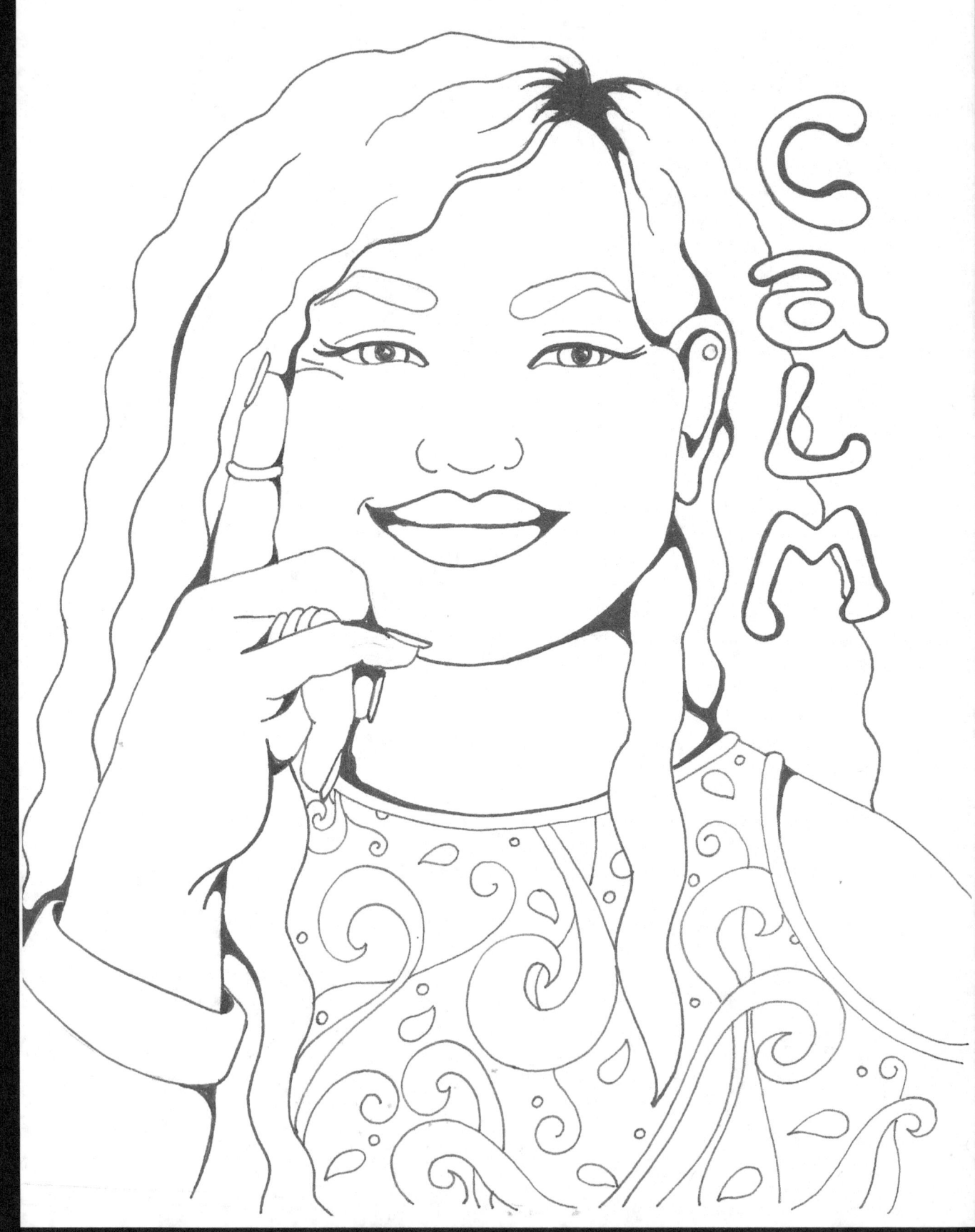

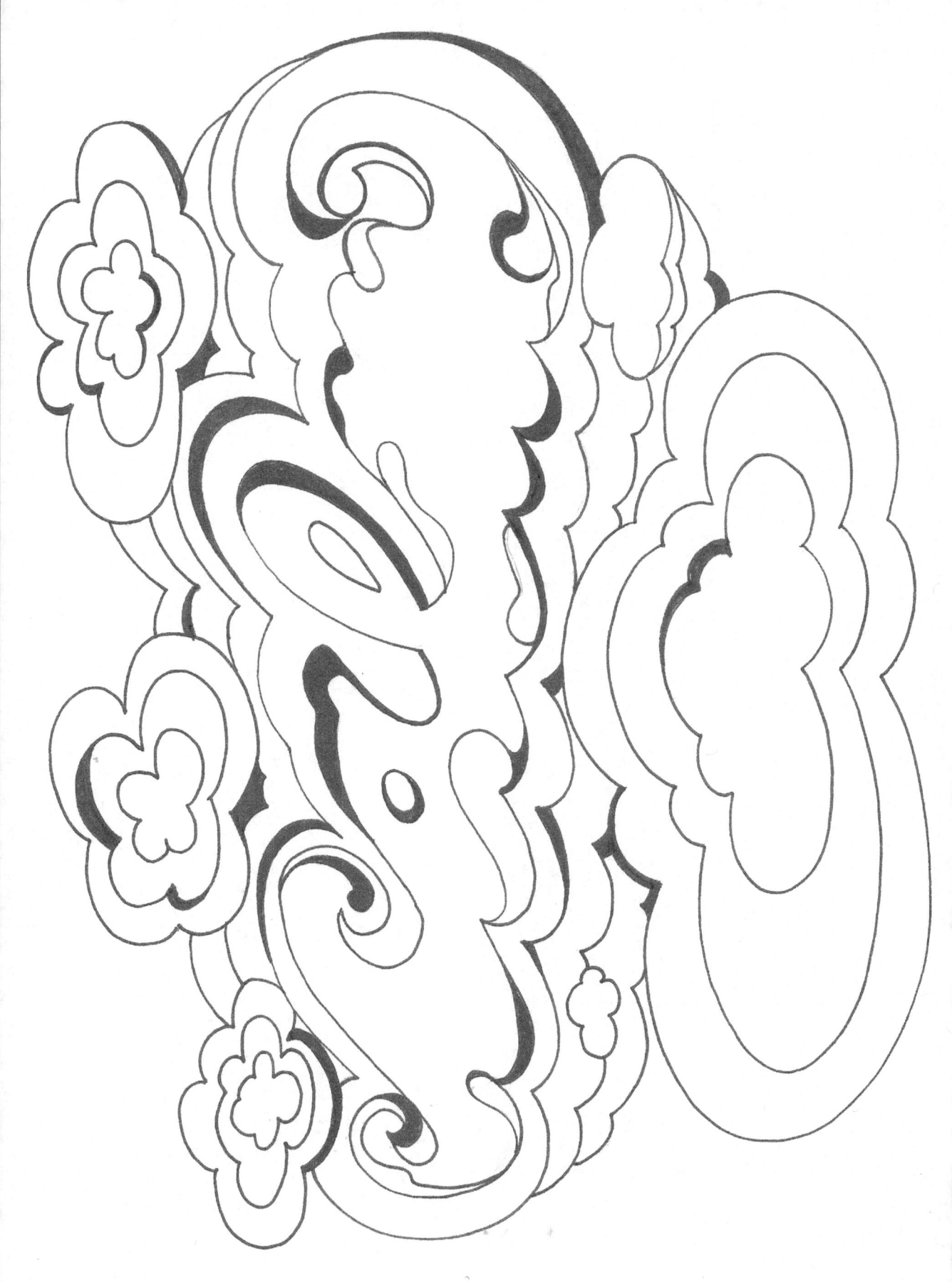

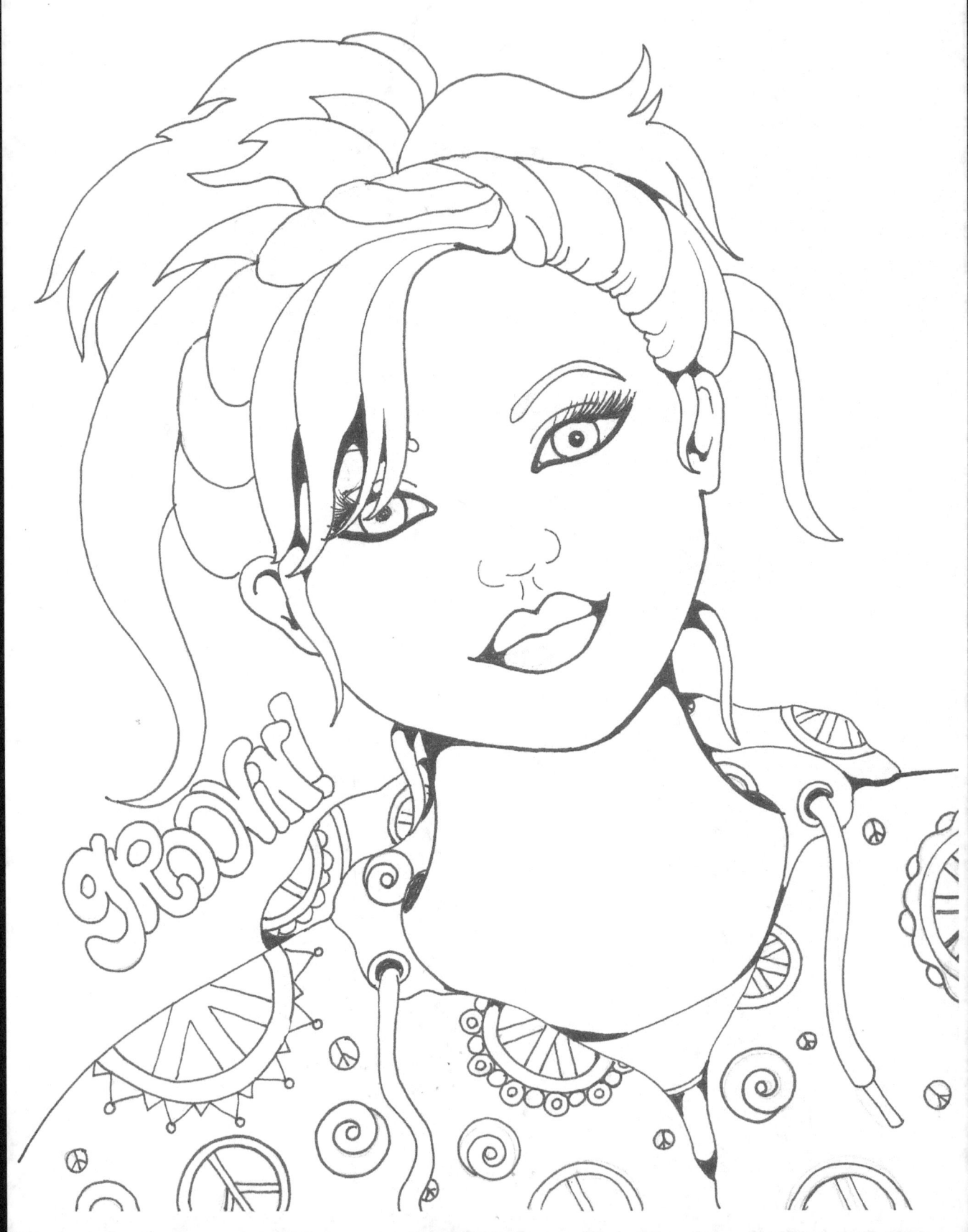

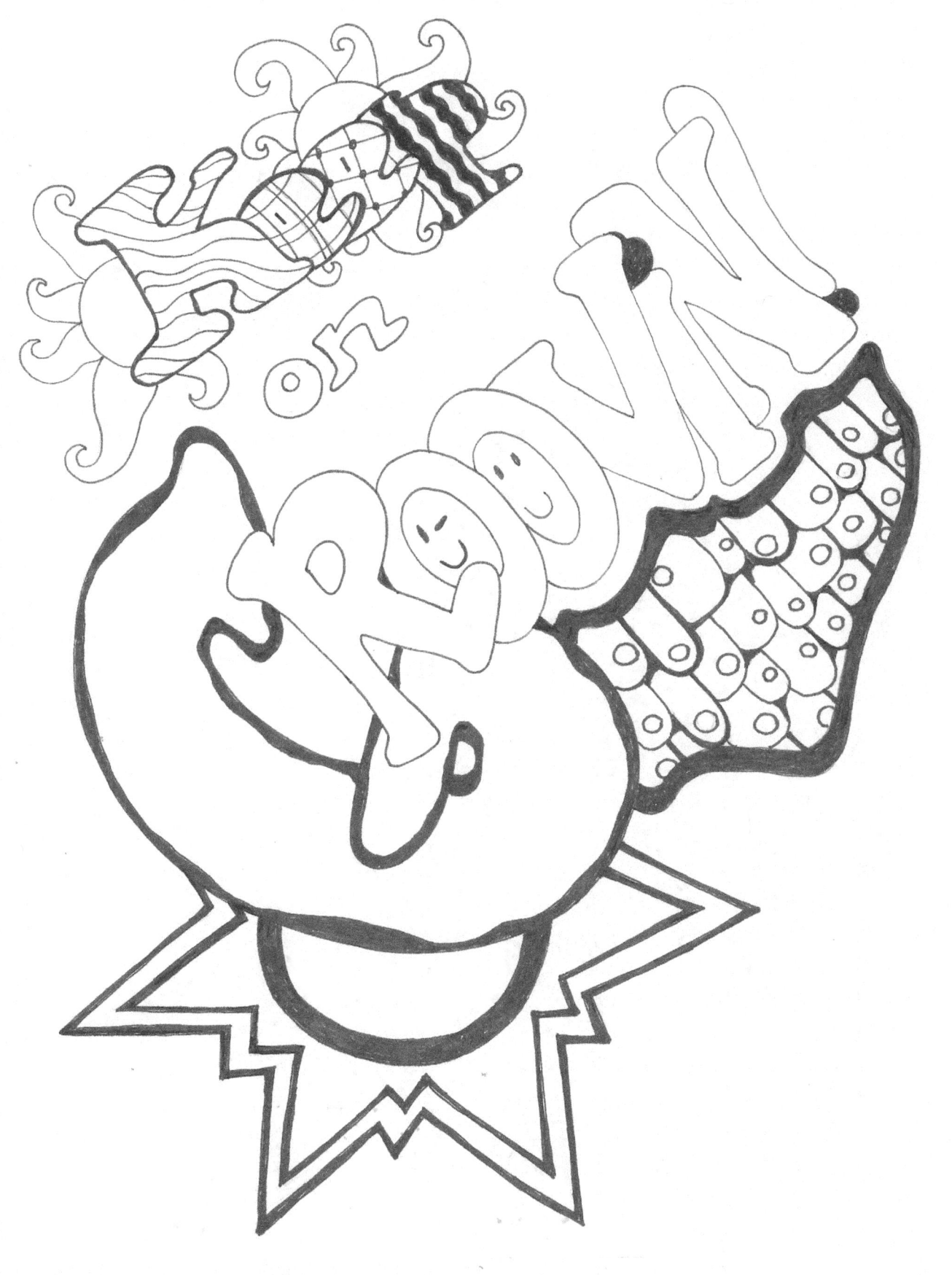

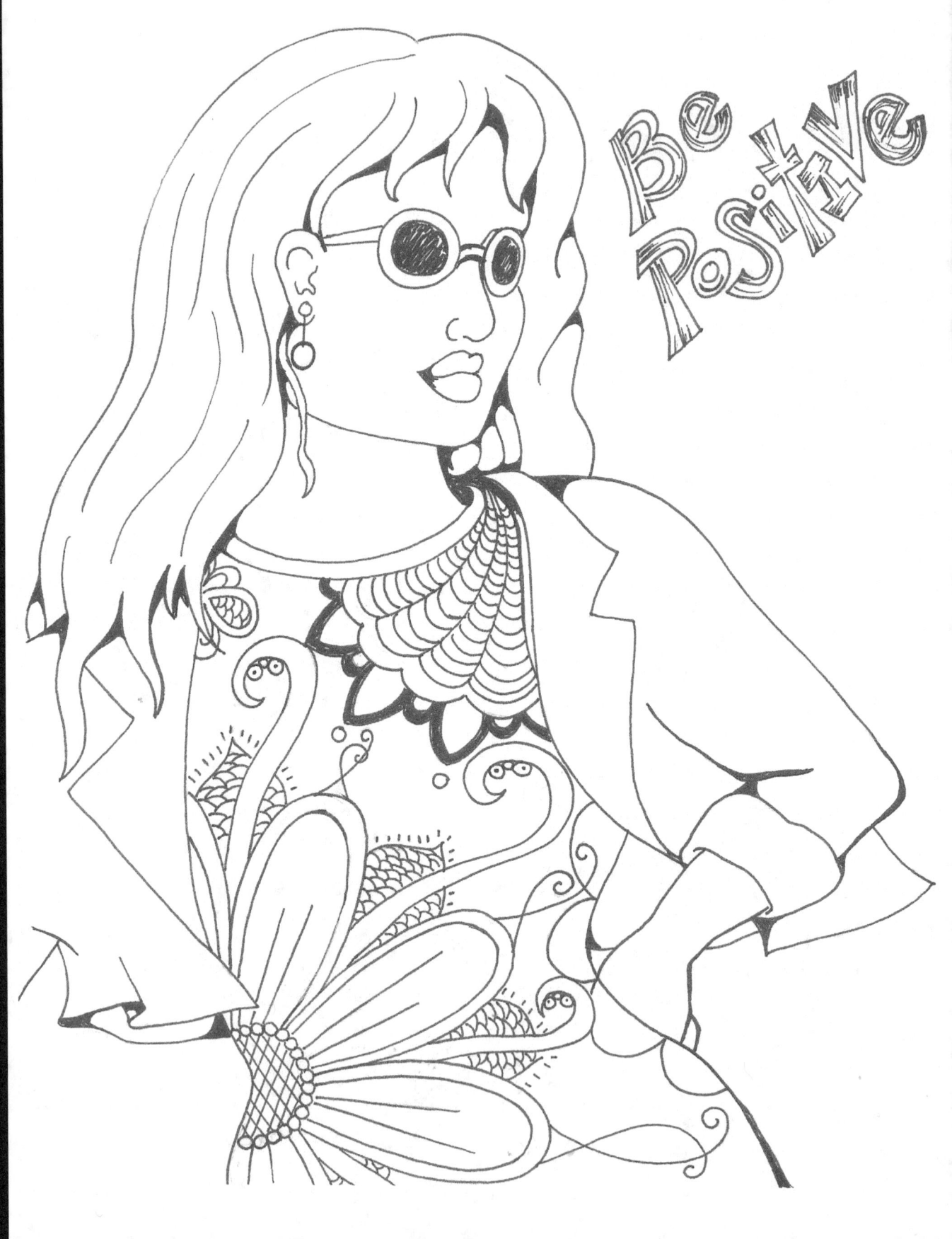

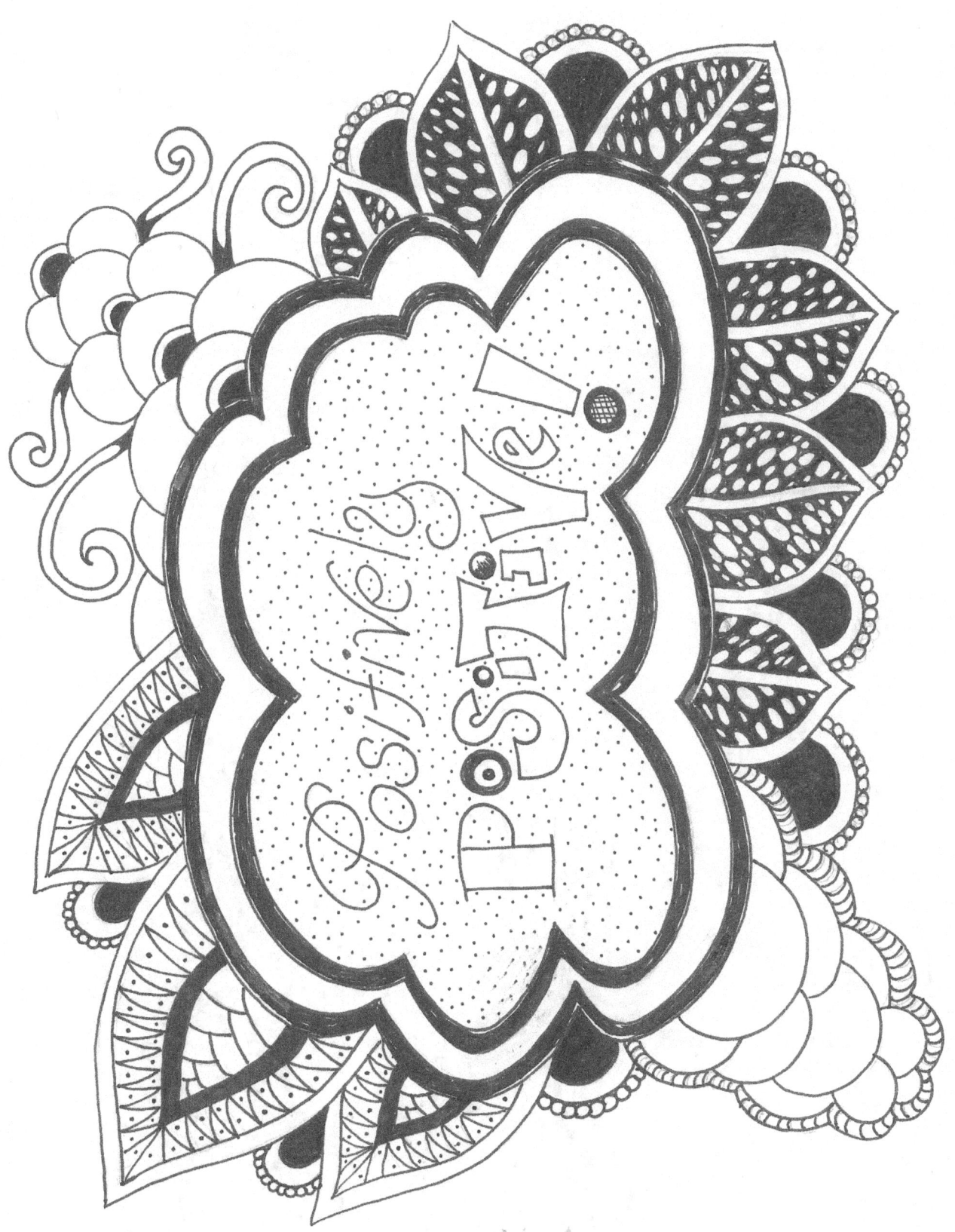

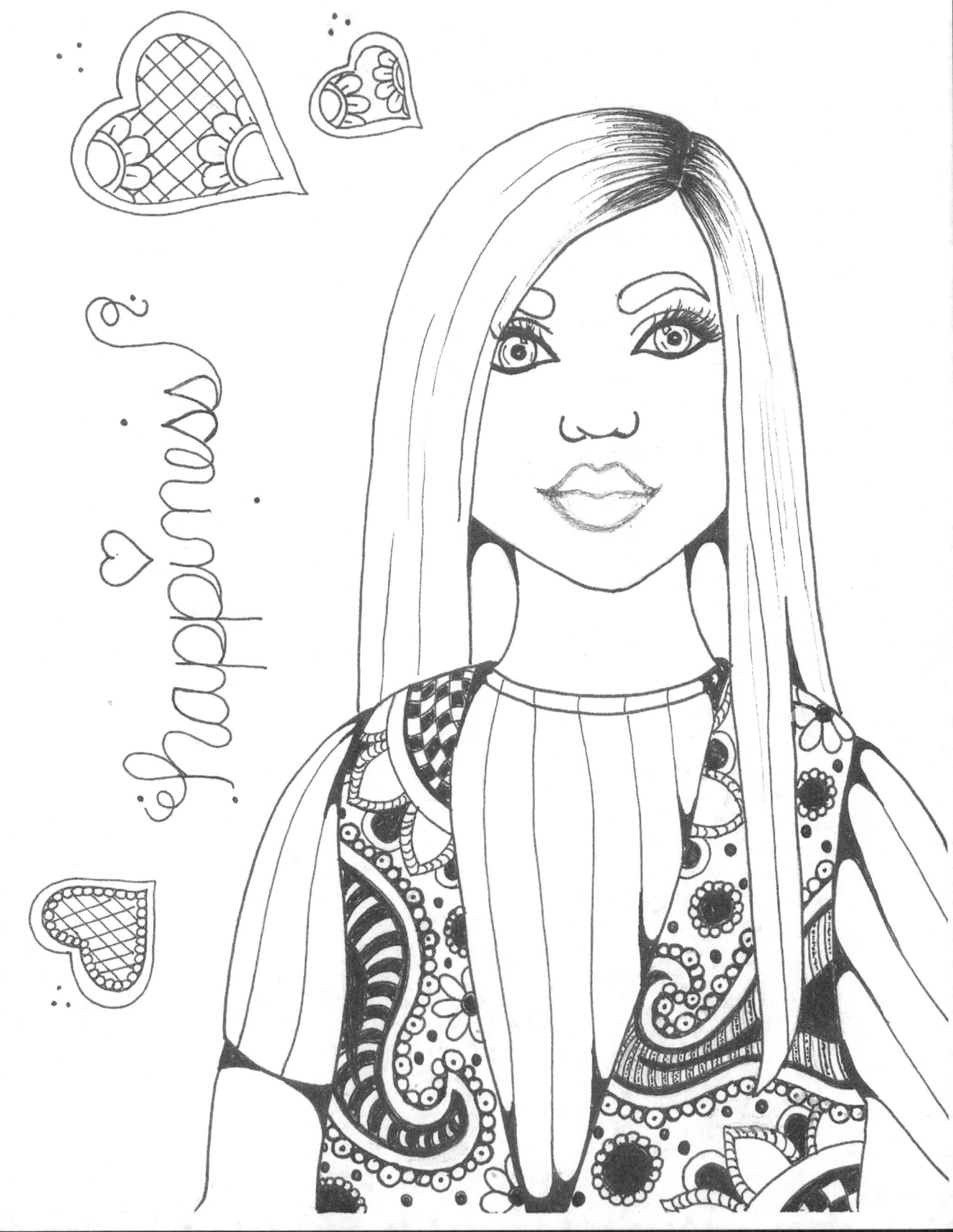

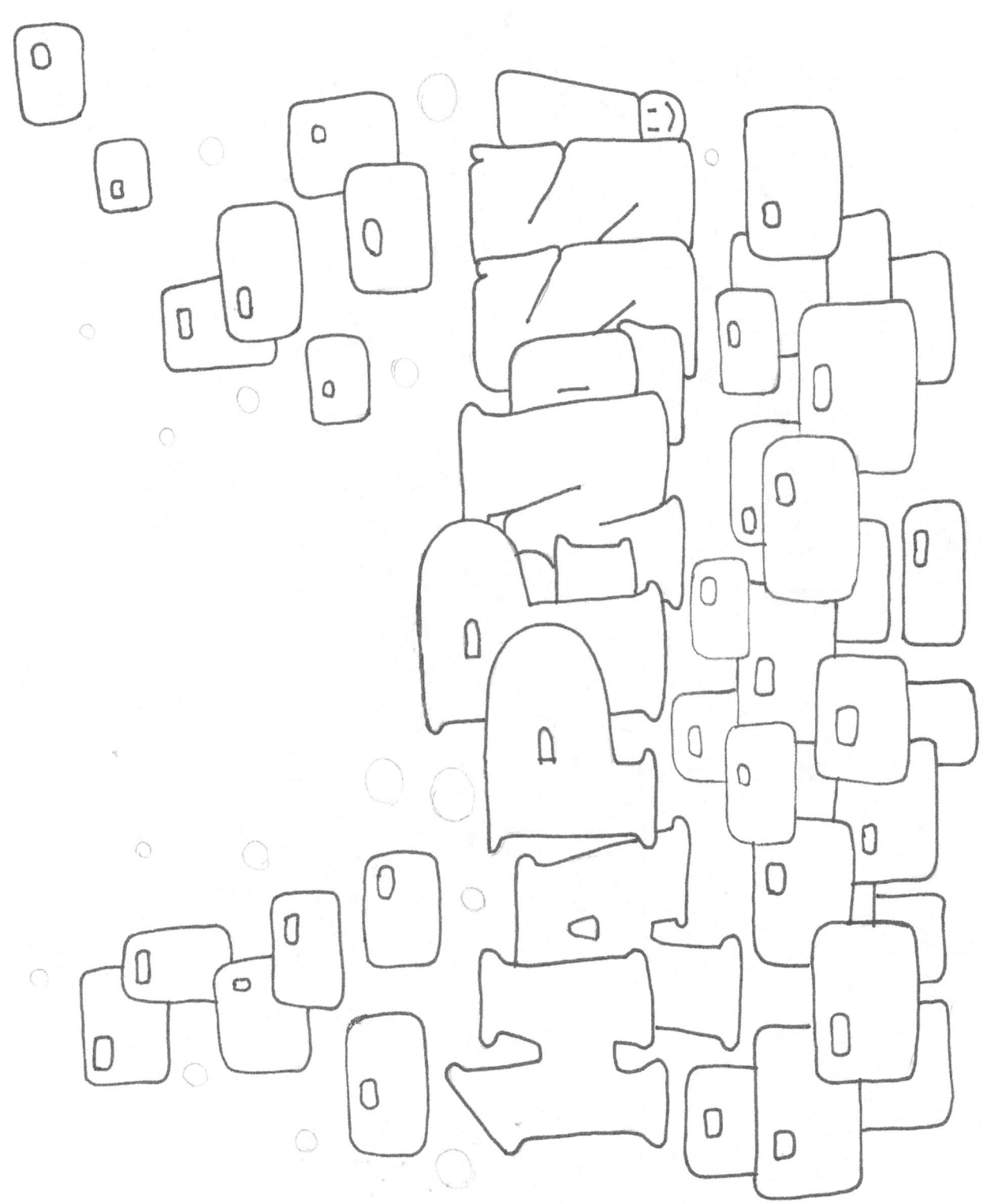

SHARE JOY

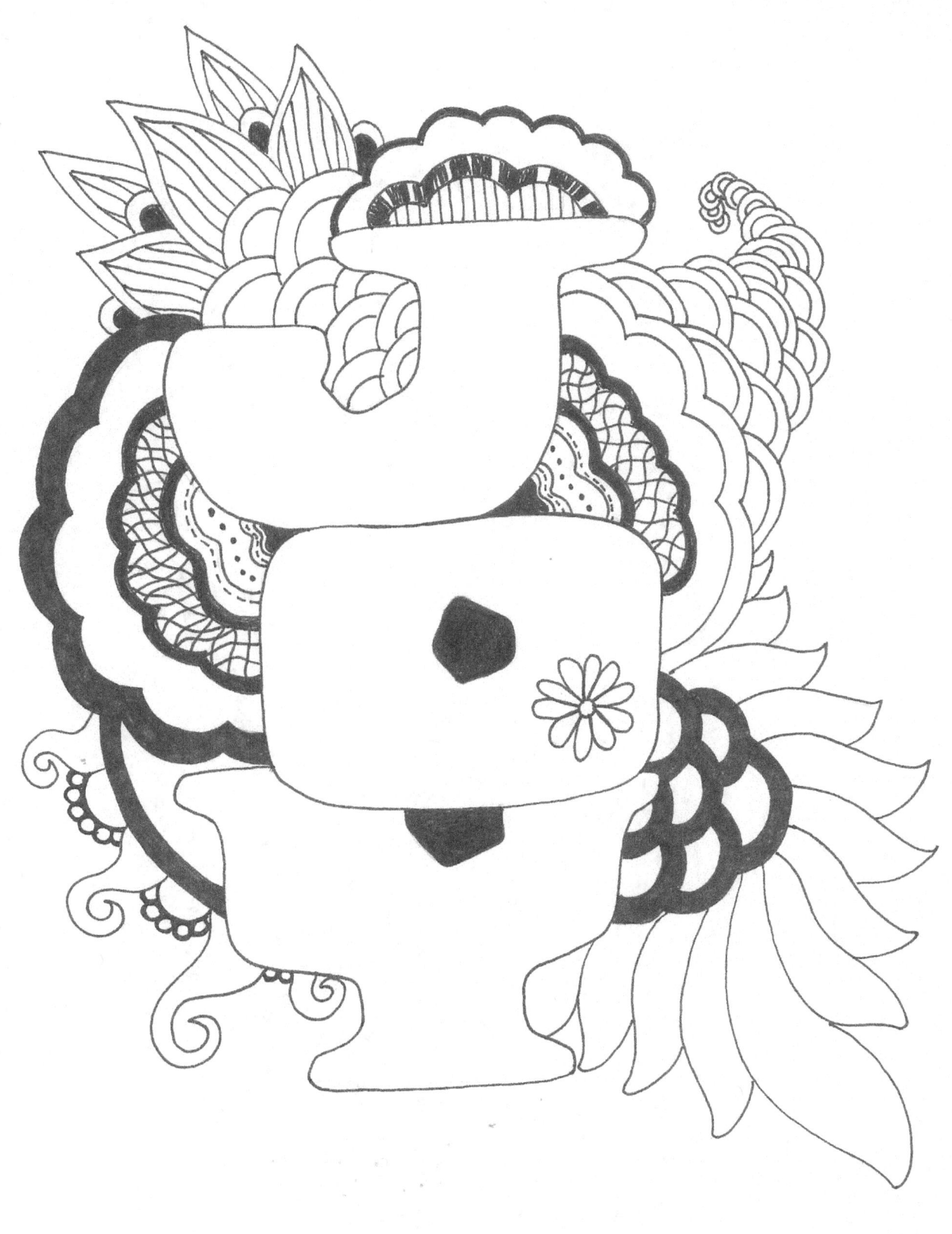

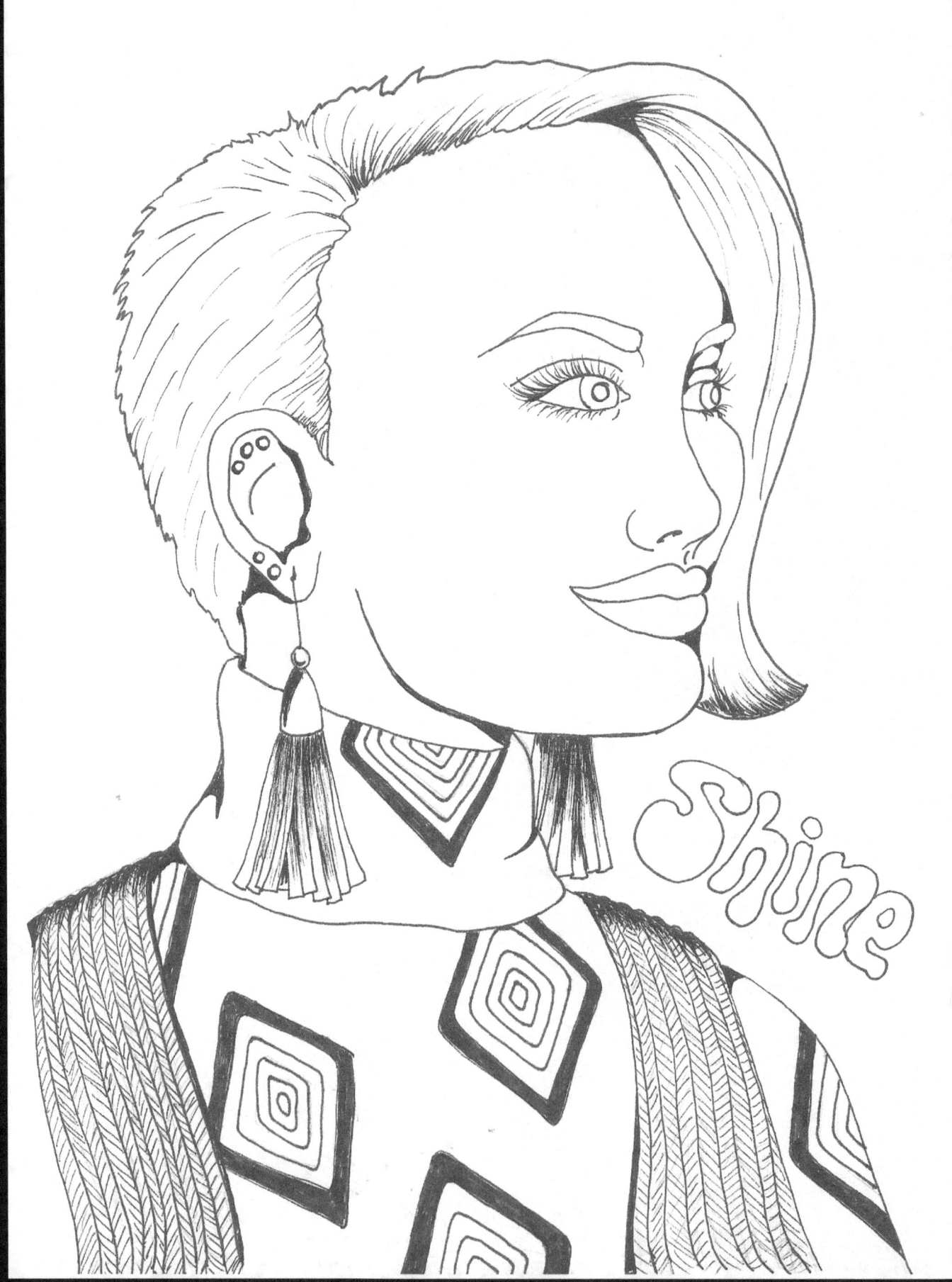

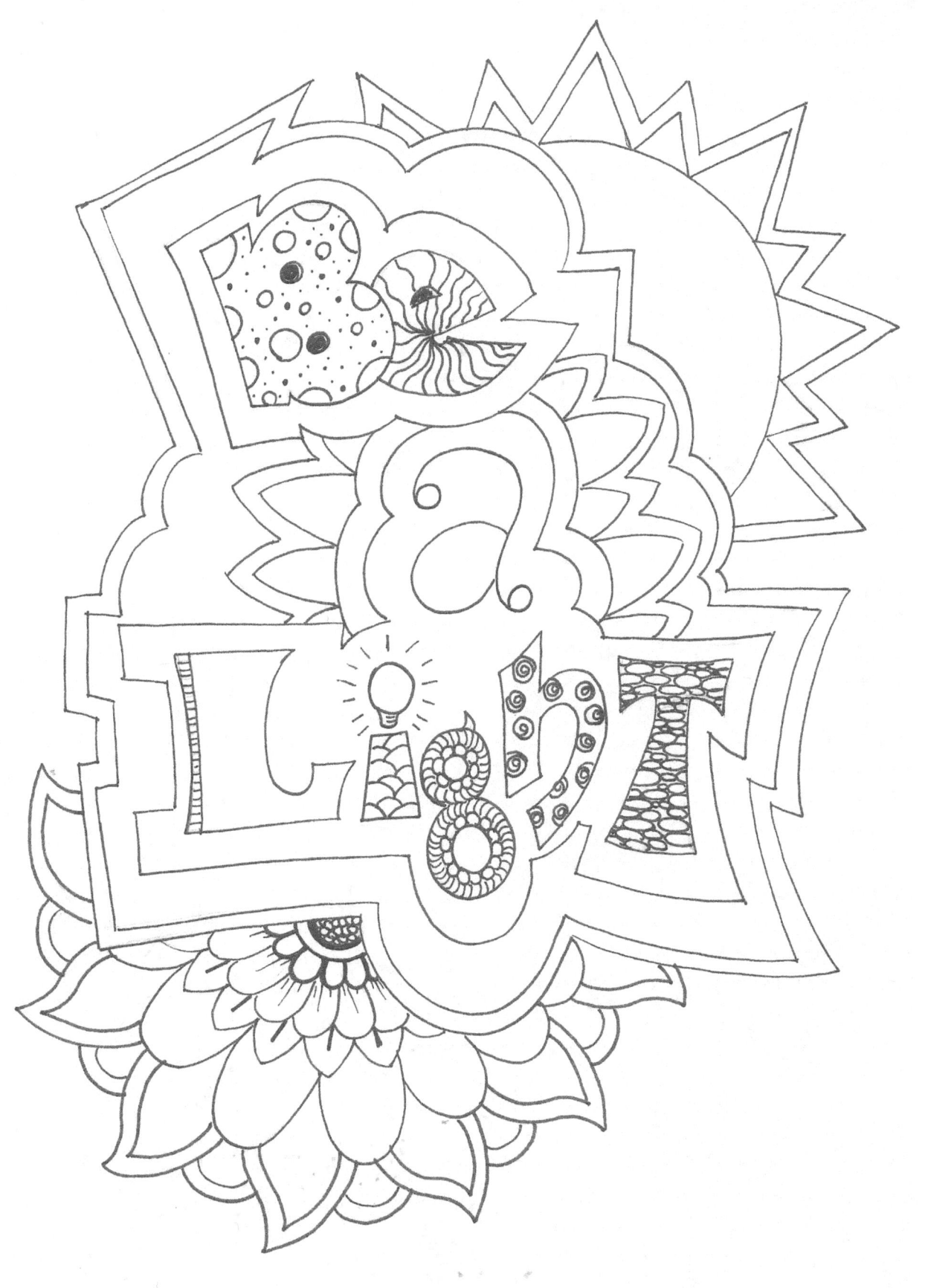

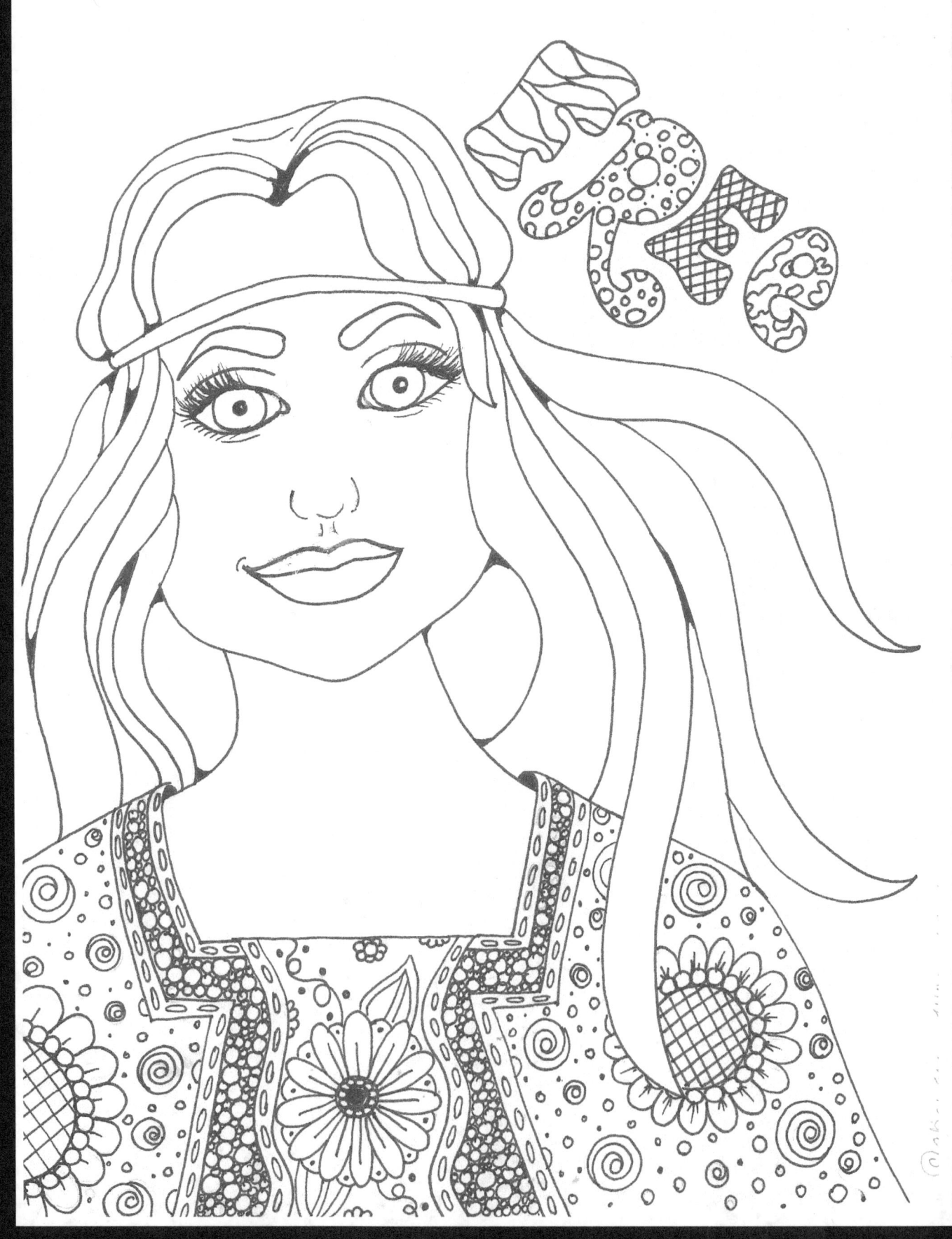

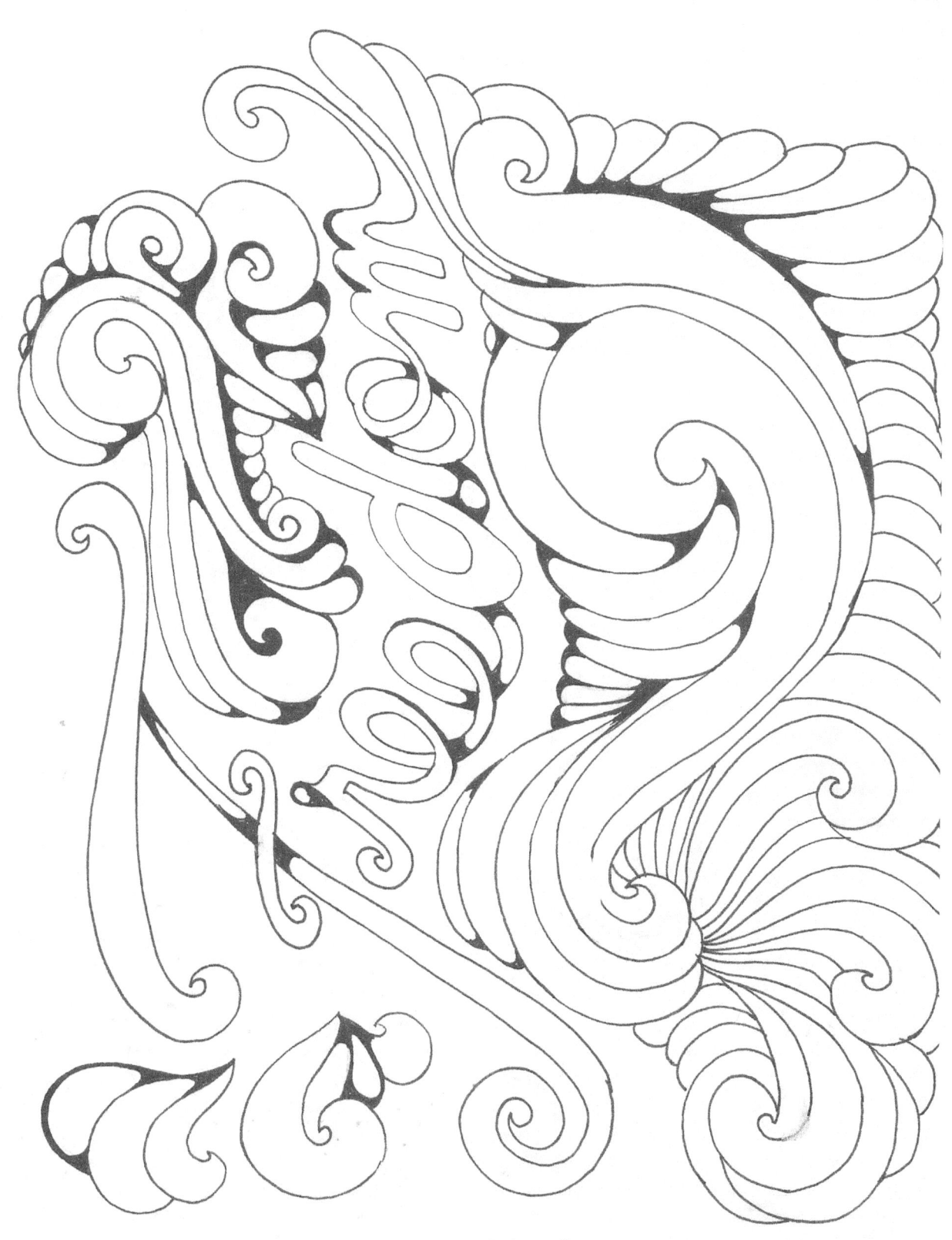

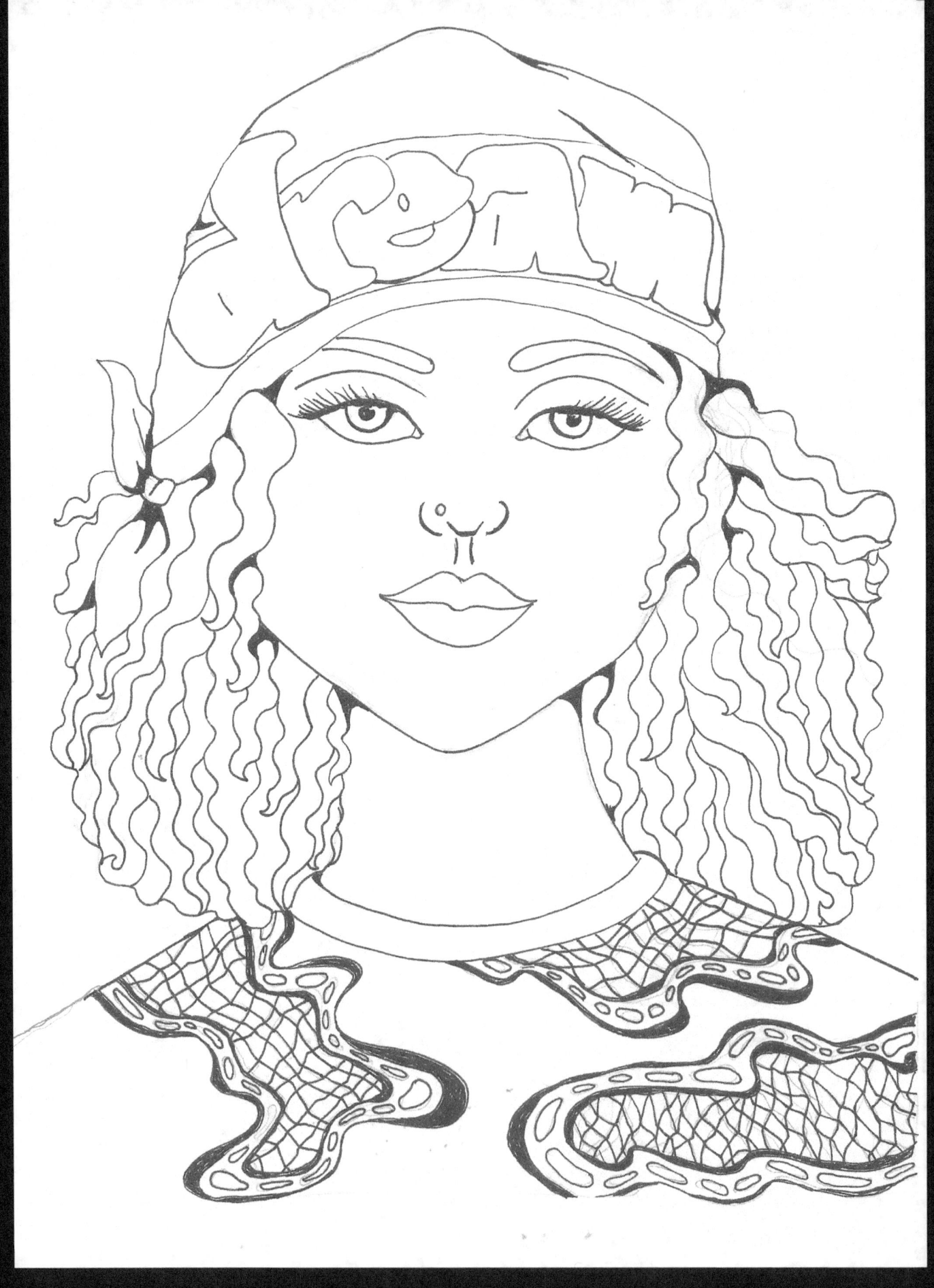

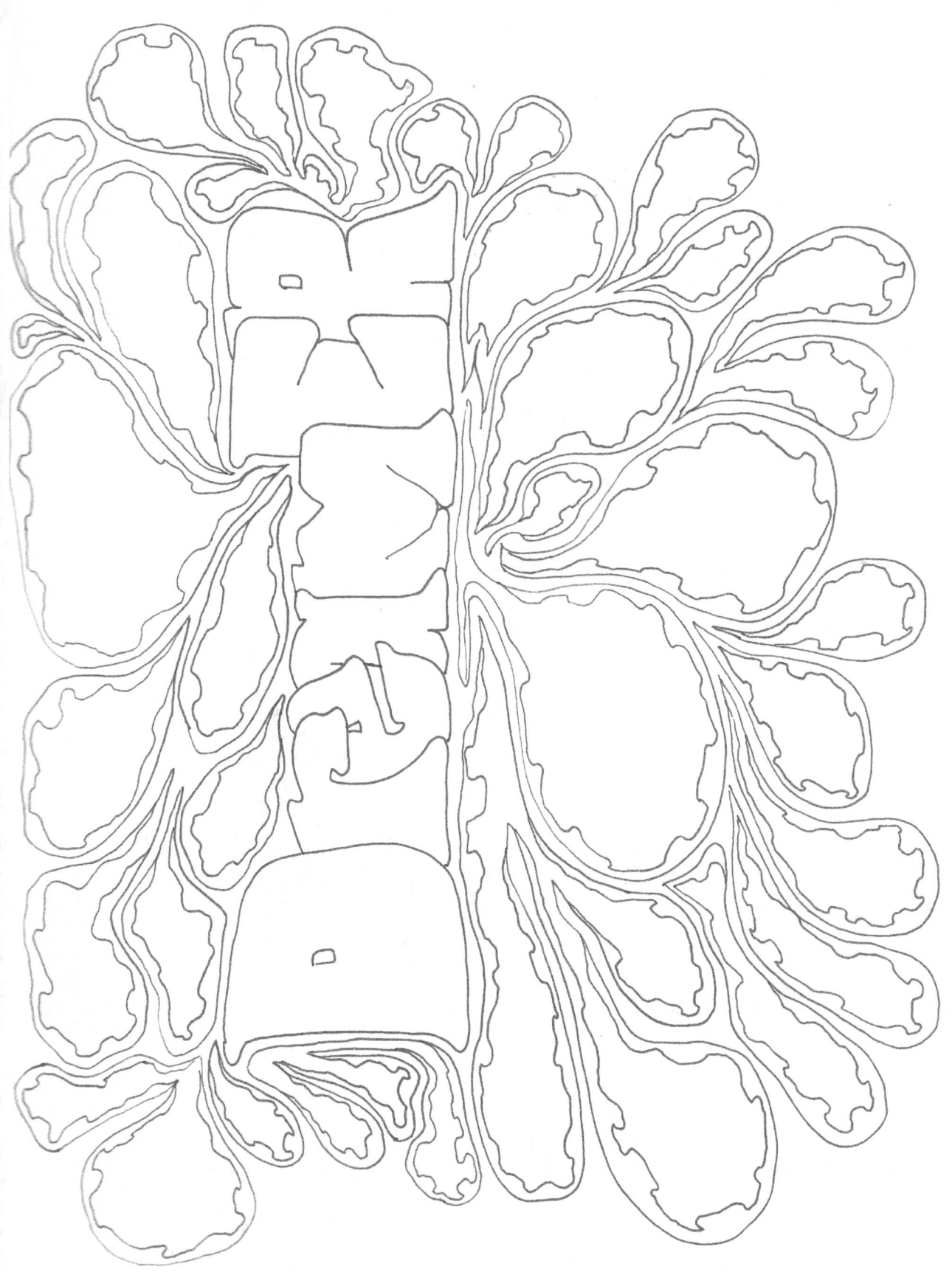

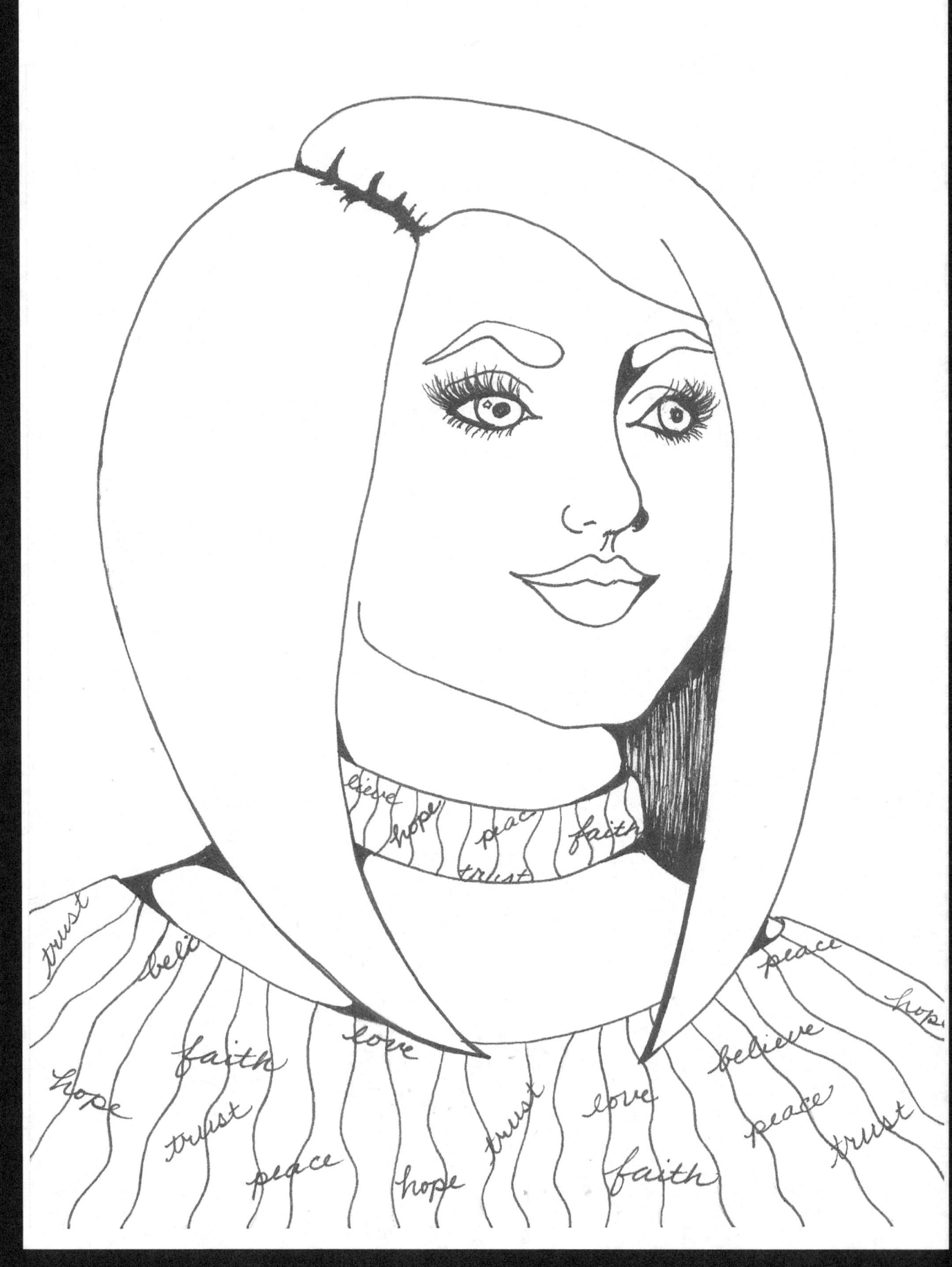

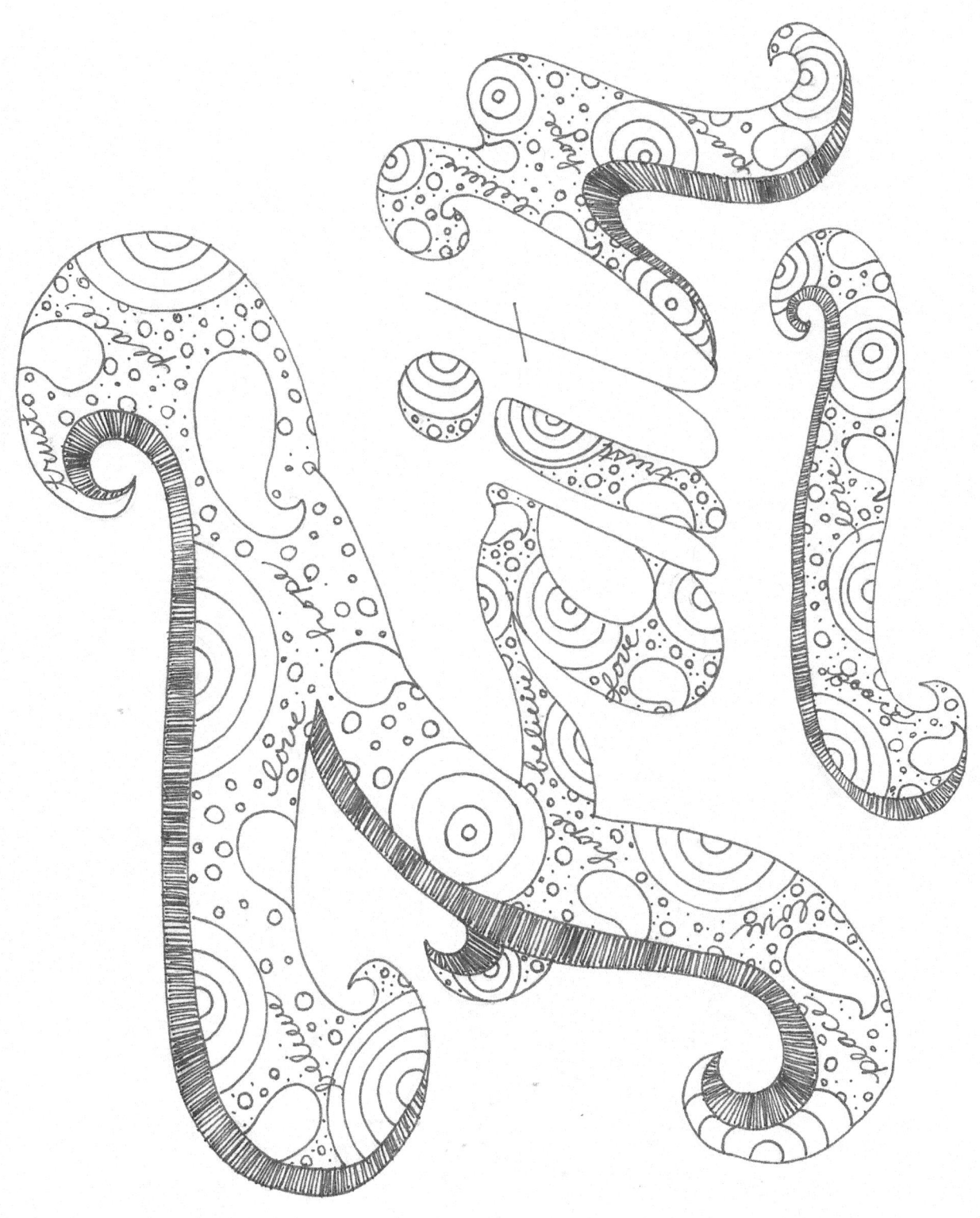

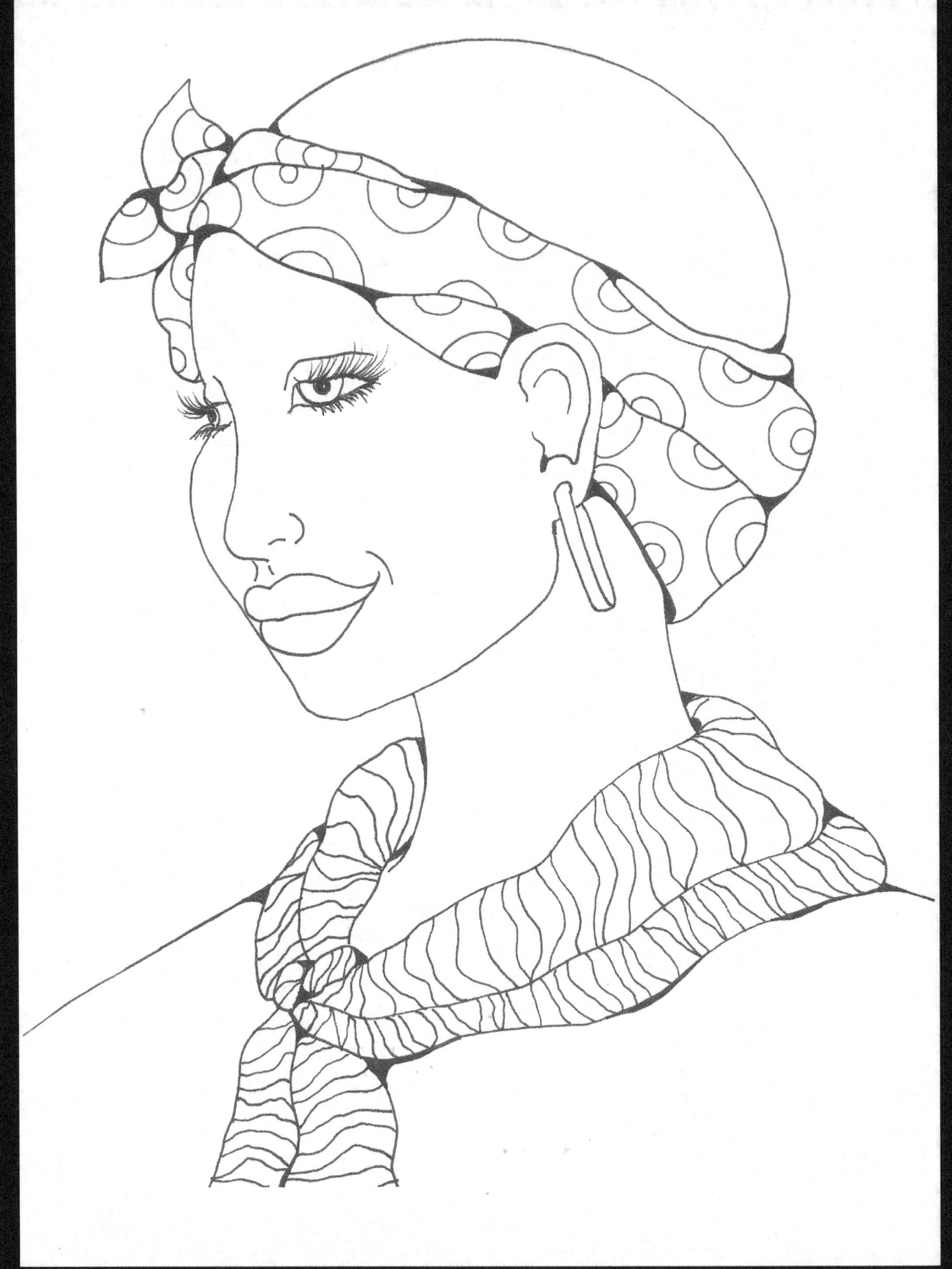

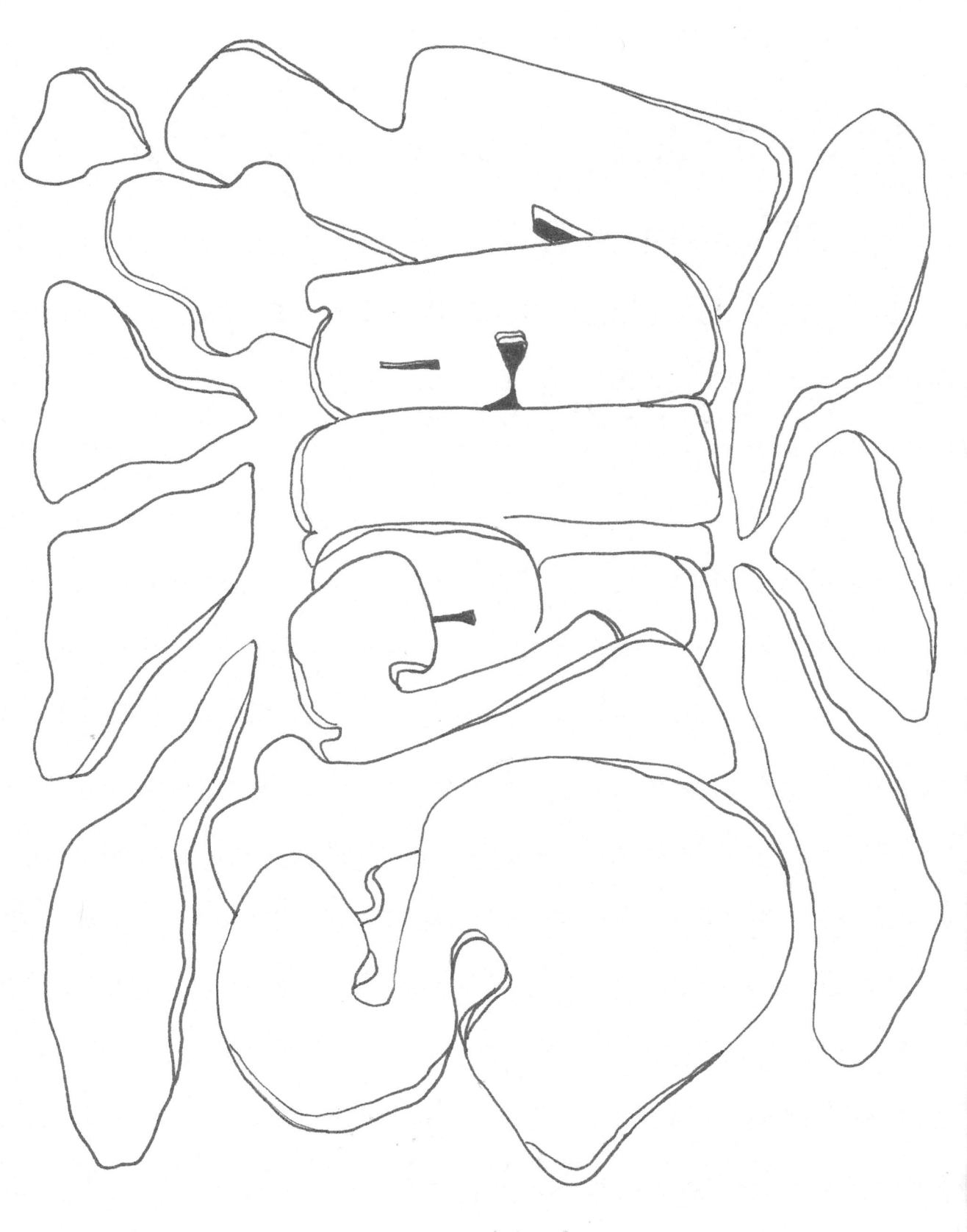

The following is an excerpt from Char Green's next coloring book, "Designed by the Word" ...coming soon!

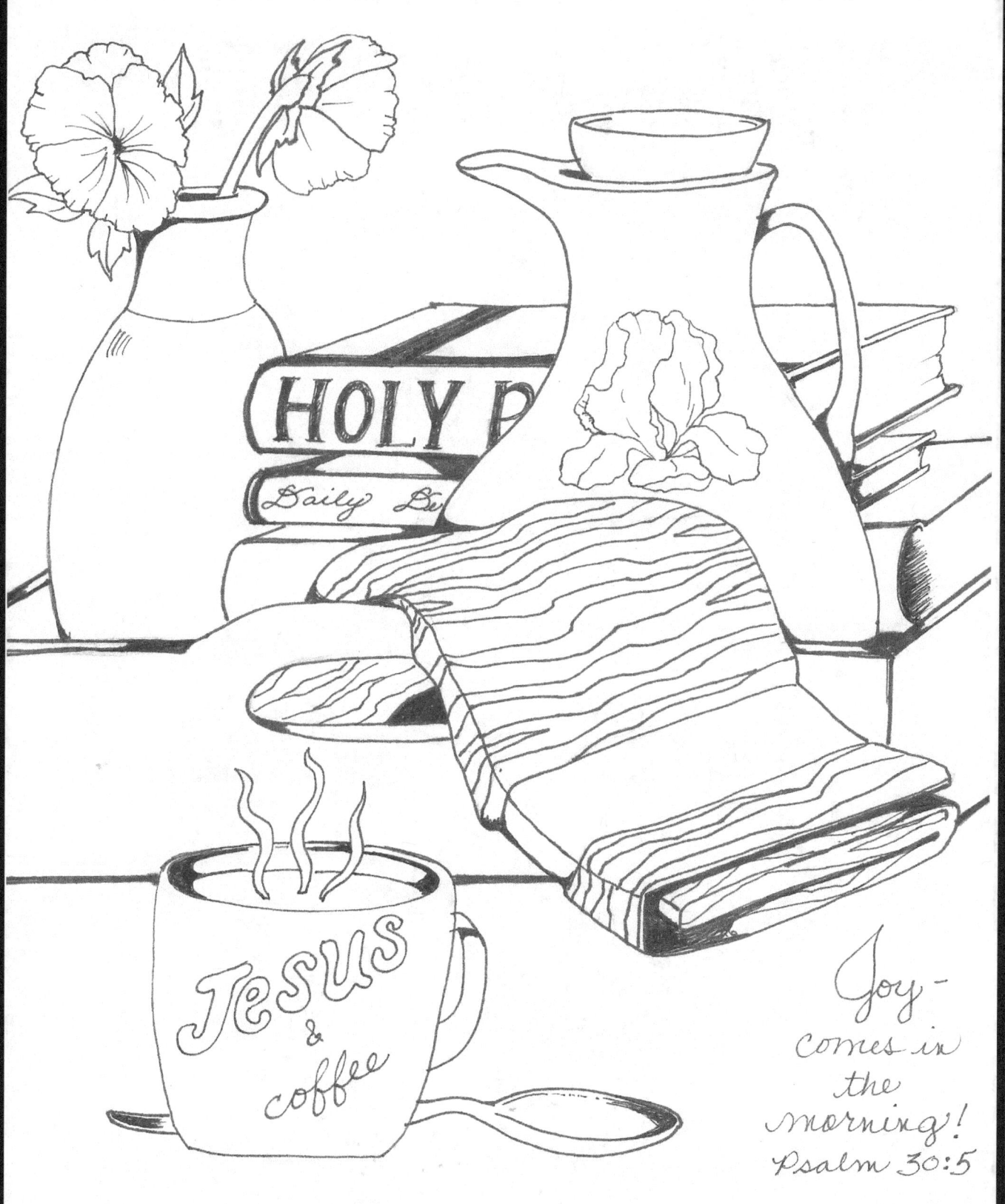

PSALM 30:5

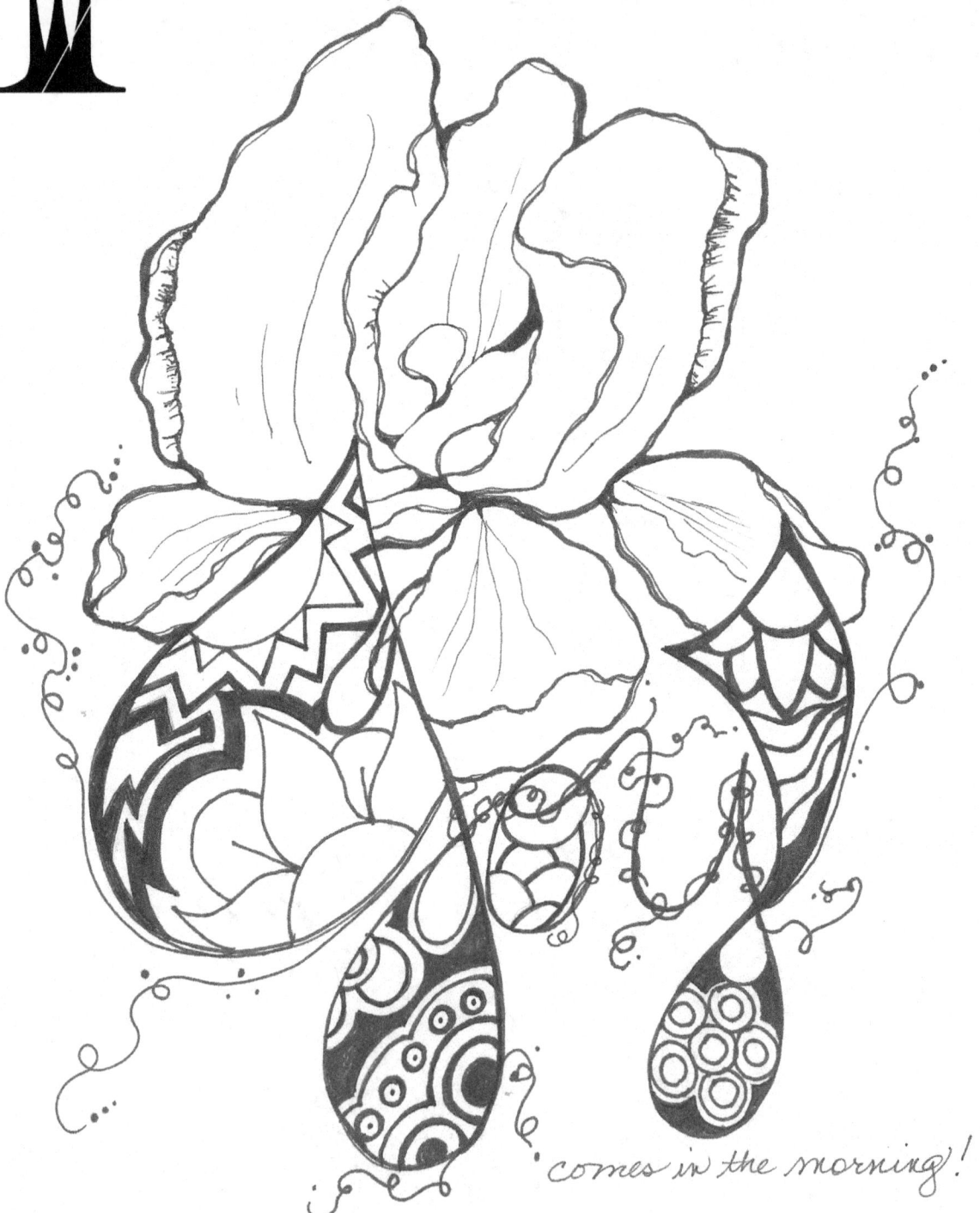

comes in the morning!